If you have ever made a mess of things
and wished for a new start then perhaps
you will understand...

Text by Lois Rock
Copyright © 1996 Lion Publishing
Illustrations copyright © 1996 Roger Langton

The author asserts the moral right
to be identified as the author of this work

Published by
Lion Publishing plc
Sandy Lane West, Oxford, England
ISBN 0 7459 3112 X
Lion Publishing
4050 Lee Vance View, Colorado Springs, CO 80918, USA
ISBN 0 7459 3112 X
Albatross Books Pty Ltd
PO Box 320, Sutherland, NSW 2232, Australia
ISBN 0 7324 0972 1

First edition 1996
10 9 8 7 6 5 4 3 2 1 0

A catalogue record for this book is available
from the British Library

Library of Congress CIP data applied for

Printed and bound in Singapore

**This retelling is based on the stories
of Jesus' life in the Bible.**

Jesus and the New Beginning

Retold by Lois Rock
Illustrations by Roger Langton

A LION BOOK

Jesus' friends were sad. Jesus had been killed by his enemies.

They didn't know what to do. So they just wept.

A rich man named Joseph took charge. "Let me take the body of Jesus," he said. "I'll bury it."

He and another of Jesus' friends took the body and laid it in a tomb rather like a cave. It had a big round stone that could be rolled in place as a door.

At sunset the weekly day of rest began. Jesus friends had to stop what they were doing.

"We'll go back after the day of rest and wrap the body properly," they said. "That will really be the last goodbye."

When that day came, the women got up very early. They went to the tomb. The stone door had been rolled away!

The tomb was empty. Where was Jesus' body?

Suddenly two people in bright shining clothes stood by them. "Why are you looking in a tomb for someone who is alive?" asked the shining people.

"Jesus is not here. God has given him new life."

The women were amazed. They went back to the others to tell their story.

"That's a silly story," they sneered.
"How dare you make up a story like
that when we're all so sad?"

But some of them went to check. The tomb was empty. One of the women, Mary, stayed there looking at it.

"I shall ask that man over there to tell me what happened," she said to herself. "I think he's the gardener. Perhaps he came here early."

When she spoke to him, he turned to look at her. "Mary," he said.

And she knew it was Jesus. He told her to go and tell people: he really was alive!

Some time after, other friends of Jesus saw him too. They had gone fishing one night, and when they came back to shore, Jesus was there to welcome them.

He was *still* their friend. They had fish for breakfast together!

Jesus had a special message for his friends: "Soon, I will go to be with God," he told them.

"You must go and tell everyone the good news about me."

And so they did. They spread the news that God loves people, just as Jesus loved people.

The news that God forgives people, just as Jesus forgave people. The news that God will give a new beginning to anyone who follows Jesus.

And the message goes on and on. It's been spreading for two thousand years. People still hear it and become friends and followers of Jesus.

They believe that one day Jesus will come back and all his friends will live with him: friends with God for ever and ever.

A Christian prayer

Dear God,
When I get things in a mess,
it's so good to know you love me.
Please give me a new beginning
and let me be your friend for ever.
Amen.